S0-AJK-646

CR ✓

APR 1 8 1995

TEACHING

TEACHING

Marjorie Eberts
Margaret Gisler

SAN DIEGO PUBLIC LIBRARY
CHILDREN'S ROOM

3 1336 03671 8956

VGM Career Horizons
a division of *NTC Publishing Group*
Lincolnwood, Illinois USA

Dedication

To all the dedicated teachers portrayed in this book
and especially to Jim Riley, our co-author on several
mathematics books for children.

Photo Credits:
Pages 1, 15, 29, and 43: Photo Network; page 57:
Jeff Ellis Photography; page 71: United Fund
(New York Jewish Guild for the Blind).

All other photographs courtesy of the authors.

Library of Congress Cataloging-in-Publication Data
Eberts, Marjorie.
    Career portraits: teaching/Marjorie Eberts, Margaret Gisler.
        p.   cm.
    ISBN0-8442-4362-0
    1. Teachers—United States—Biography.   2 Teaching.   I. Gisler, Margaret.
II. Title.
LB1775.2.E24 1995
371.1'00973—dc20   93-47956
                                                                CIP

Published by VGM Career Horizons, a division of NTC Publishing Group
4255 West Touhy Avenue
Lincolnwood (Chicago), Illinois 60646-1975, U.S.A.
© 1995 by NTC Publishing Group. All rights reserved.
No part of this book may be reproduced, stored in a retrieval system,
or transmitted in any form or by any means,
electronic, mechanical, photocopying, recording or otherwise,
without the prior permission of NTC Publishing Group.
Manufactured in the United States of America.

4 5 6 7 8 9 ML 9 8 7 6 5 4 3 2 1

Contents

The decent docent doesn't doze;
He teaches standing on his toes.
His student doesn't doze and does,
And that's what teaching is and was.

—*What Cheer,* 1945

Introduction

Teaching is helping other people learn. It is not a new profession. Scholars like Aristotle, Plato, and Socrates were teachers. If you have the same desire to help future generations of children learn, then teaching is a career you should consider.

Reading this book will give you important information about a teaching career. Each chapter will tell you what it is like to be a teacher at a certain grade level. You will have the opportunity to meet teachers and get their personal feelings about their jobs. You will find out what happens on the job, the pleasures and pressures of teaching, the rewards, the pay, the perks, and the education you need. But more importantly, by reading this book you will discover whether you possess the aptitudes, skills, and personality needed to succeed in teaching. As you read the book, you will be amazed at the number of famous people throughout history who have selected teaching as their profession.

PRESCHOOL OR KINDERGARTEN TEACHER

Just imagine being a child's first teacher! As a preschool or kindergarten teacher, you will be introducing young children to the world of letters and numbers, opening their eyes to the joys of art and music, and helping them learn about themselves and the world around them. You will be challenged daily to provide interesting, exciting, and motivating ideas that will make young children want to learn. In your role as a preschool or kindergarten teacher, you will also be a nurse, a referee for fights, a playground director, a mother or father, and a friend.

1

What it's like to be a preschool or kindergarten teacher

You will be a very important person in the lives of every one of your young students. You will also be a giant in a world of miniature tables, chairs, easels, and playthings. At times, you will sit and read stories, but you will never be still for long. Children will be learning the most important lessons of life in your classroom such as sharing, respecting others, telling the truth, and trying to do their best at all times.

Let's find out what happens on the job

Long before the first child ever enters the classroom, preschool and kindergarten teachers have made lesson plans, selected story books, mixed paints, and set up craft projects. From the minute children walk through the classroom door, the teacher is busy greeting, guiding, assisting, and encouraging each student as well as organizing group activities. The teacher also spots children who are not feeling well, listens to complaints, and comforts the sad or injured child. At all times, the teacher is trying to help the children grow mentally, socially, and emotionally.

The pleasures and pressures of the job

Each day is satisfying for preschool and kindergarten teachers because young children develop and learn so rapidly. You can see a shy child turn into an active member of a group or a less skilled child master a task like drawing a circle. As a teacher of young children, you will be constantly challenged to find new and innovative techniques to motivate each child to learn in his or her special way. Working with young children is a job that is rewarding, challenging, hectic, and even tiring but never dull or boring.

The rewards, the pay, and the perks

Being a preschool or kindergarten teacher is immensely rewarding because your students really show their affection for you, and you feel their energy and enthusiasm for learning. The average salary for both preschool and kindergarten teachers with state certification is approximately $32,000 per year. This salary is usually based upon a teacher's education level and experience. The biggest perks of being a teacher at this level are the relatively short hours you work and having time off for all major holidays plus a long summer vacation.

Getting started

Most states require a state license to teach. Kindergarten and pre-school teachers usually have college or university degrees in early childhood education plus the necessary licenses. However, some preschool teachers only have associate (two-year) degrees in early childhood education or child development. Other preschool teachers enter the field through the Child Development Associate Program, which trains teachers on the job. You can also study to become a preschool or kindergarten teacher through the American Montessori Society.

Climbing the career ladder

Both preschool and kindergarten teachers can climb the career ladder to become lead teachers, directors, or even principals. Some preschool teachers go on to start their own schools. Other preschool teachers can enter the management side of companies that run a number of preschools. Preschool and kinder-garten teachers can also go on to government positions. They can even decide to become college professors and teach students how to be preschool or kindergarten teachers.

Now decide if teaching preschool or kindergarten is right for you

How truly interested are you in children of this age? Are you going to want to spend considerable time in college or a special training program finding out all you can about young children? Think also about how willing you are to spend all your working hours with children. If young children are not your absolutely favorite age group, you might want to find out more in later chapters of this book about teaching older children.

Things you can do to get a head start

Here are some places where you can gain experience working with young children.

- Neighborhood (baby-sitter)
- Summer camp programs
- Daycare centers
- Youth organization programs
- Sunday school

In high school, try to take as many courses as you can that relate to early childhood learning. Look for courses like cadet teaching, family living, and psychology.

Let's Meet...

Cathy Johnson
Preschool Teacher

Cathy has been a preschool teacher for the past 15 years. She especially enjoys the variety of teaching young children of several different ages.

What first attracted you to a career in teaching?

I have always enjoyed working with young children. It must be a family trait, as my mother taught first grade for 49 years. I saw how much my mother loved her job and believed she was making a real contribution to children's lives.

Did you need any special schooling or training?

The school where I teach does not require its teachers to have a degree in early childhood education. However, a teaching degree is required, and one in elementary education is preferred. My own background includes a kindergarten endorsement and a master's degree in early childhood education.

Do you use the knowledge/skills you learned in school on the job?

Yes, I most certainly do. I was very fortunate to have several very enthusiastic teachers in college who had taught preschool and kindergarten. Many of the projects that I did for their classes were so helpful that I am still using them in my teaching today.

What special skills do you need to be a good teacher?

A good preschool teacher must be patient and firm with his or her young students, yet at the same time loving and very flexible. Teachers also need to have an excellent understanding of children and how they develop and what their abilities are at each age level.

What are your favorite and least favorite things about your job?

Because I love my job so much, I have so many more favorite things about my job than drawbacks. Some of the reasons I enjoy my job are:

- It is never boring: there is so much variety.
- I enjoy meeting the children's families.
- Children at this age constantly make you feel good because they genuinely like you.
- The shorter hours are very appealing.
- Our preschool is so nice.
- Young children are open and spontaneous.

The few drawbacks of my job include:

- The teachers at our preschool do not have any health or medical insurance.
- This job is physically tiring.
- I tend to pick up ailments.

Cathy Johnson's Week

It seems like no two days are alike. I teach a class of four-year-olds three days a week.

On Monday, we have an extended day, and the children bring their lunches and stay until 2:00.

This year I am lucky enough to have Tuesday off.

Our Wednesday and Friday sessions are from 9:00 to 11:30.

On Thursday, I teach a morning class of two-year-olds from 9:30 to 11:30 and a kindergarten enrichment program from 12:15 to 2:30.

Every year, my schedule changes as the school enrollment varies.

Let's Meet...

Jackie McVey
Kindergarten Teacher

Jackie has taught kindergarten for seven years. Her happiest moments on the job come when a struggling student finally succeeds in doing a task.

What first attracted you to a career in early childhood education?

I taught Sunday school when my children were young and found that young children are fun to work with! I knew I would enjoy teaching because this experience had been so rewarding.

Did you need any special schooling or training?

I needed a college degree plus additional hours in education to be certified. My college courses laid the foundation on which I have built from experience gained on the job. Many of the skills and techniques that I use in the classroom I have learned from other teachers. And I keep taking classes and workshops and attending conferences so I can learn even more.

What special skills do you need?

Of course, kindergarten teachers need to like working with children, but they also need to like working with parents. The relationship between parents and teachers is so important in helping young children do well in school.

At what type of kindergarten do you work?

I work at a cooperative kindergarten, which is a school operated by parents. The parents take turns acting as aides in the classroom and suggesting interesting activities for the class. Last year, my class went to a pro football locker room because one of the fathers is a professional football player.

What is the most difficult part of your job?

Being very well organized is difficult for me. Teachers are required to keep track of many resources. I frequently have to look for things!

Describe a happy moment on the job.

Kindergarten teachers are lucky because they have so many happy moments. Every day the children give you warm hugs and friendly smiles.

What do like most and least about your job?

The best times are those when kids who feel challenged and keep trying finally say, "I can." I also enjoy the warm affection young children give so freely to significant adults. The least appealing part of my job is the fact that a teacher's job is never done! There is always more that I want to do, but time simply does not permit me to do it.

Kindergarten A.M. Schedule

9:30-9:50	**Greetings** **Show and Tell** **Calendar** **Writer's Suitcase**
9:50-10:15	**Choice Time: Journals,** **Computer, Puzzles,** **Self Activities**
10:15-10:30	**Multi-purpose Room:** **Games, Bathroom/Drinks**
10:30-10:45	**Class Meeting:** **Goals/Objectives**
10:45-11:25	**Centers: Math, Craft,** **Language Arts**
11:25-11:35	**Circle** **Shared Reading**
11:35-11:55	**Free Time**
11:55-12:00	**Dismissal**

Success Stories

Maria Montessori

Maria Montessori, an Italian doctor, believed strongly that young children should learn first through their senses—seeing, hearing, feeling, tasting, and smelling—and then with their minds. This was a brand-new idea in 1907 when Maria opened her first preschool called Casa dei Bambini, which means Children's House in Italian. In Maria's school, children were free to move around and touch things in the classroom and pick whatever they wanted to do. They did not have to stay in their seats as young schoolchildren of that time were forced to do. Her teaching methods helped young children learn how to learn by themselves. These methods were so successful that they are still being used in Montessori schools throughout the world.

Bill Cosby

Do you realize that Bill Cosby, the actor and creator of the Emmy-winning program "The Cosby Show," has a doctorate in education? A doctorate is the highest degree that a university gives to a student. While Bill was working on his doctorate degree, he studied the uses and effects of electronic devices, including television, on children's education. Bill uses his acting skills on television to teach young children throughout the United States. You may have seen him on "The Electric Company" teaching young children to read or on "Sesame Street" teaching children to say letters and numbers. Even his cartoons "Fat Albert" and the "Cosby Kids" have an educational message.

Find Out More

You and young children

Not everyone has the personality to be a preschool or kindergarten teacher. Take this quiz to find out if you have the same traits as most successful kindergarten teachers.

Do you enjoy being with young children?

Are you patient with young children?

Can you keep your cool when things go wrong?

Do you get satisfaction from helping others?

Do you have a pleasant-sounding voice?

Do you have a high energy level?

Are you able to adapt to a new situation quickly?

Will you be able to control a group of young children?

Are you an imaginative and creative person? Do you enjoy reading children's stories?

Do you enjoy playing with children?

Do you enjoy spontaneous activities?

Do you like doing art, music, crafts?

The more "yes" answers you have, the better suited you are to a career in teaching young children.

Find out more about teaching preschool and kindergarten

By contacting the following organizations, you can find out more about teaching young children.

American Montessori Society
150 Fifth Ave.
New York, NY 10011

Association for Childhood
  Education International
11141 Georgia Ave.
Wheaton, MD 20902

Council for Early Childhood
  Professional Recognition
1718 Connecticut Ave. N.W.,
  Suite 500
Washington, DC 20009

National Association for the
  Education of Young Children
1834 Connecticut Ave. N.W.
Washington, DC 20009

National Council for Accreditation
  of Teacher Education
2010 Massachusetts Ave. N.W.,
  Suite 200
Washington, DC 20036

ELEMENTARY

TEACHER

T he eager first grader wants to learn to read, write, and handle numbers. And with each higher grade level, the elementary teacher helps children learn more and more about the world. It's very exciting to teach children about the pioneers who crossed the country in covered wagons, to introduce them to multiplication and even long division, and to help them learn geography, history, science, English, and health. Today's elementary school teachers even have computers and calculators in the classroom to help children learn.

You won't just be teaching subjects to children in elementary school; you will also be helping them grow socially and emotionally. Think about the satisfaction you will have from helping children learn how to work together.

What it's like to be an elementary school teacher

Most elementary school teachers stay with one class all day teaching the children several subjects. As an elementary school teacher, you will plan lessons, prepare tests, grade papers, make out report cards, meet with parents, and attend faculty meetings and conferences. You will also assign lessons, give tests, hear oral presentations, and oversee special projects with your students. Your most important task, however, is to build upon your children's desire to learn and help them remain enthusiastic learners.

Let's find out what happens on the job

Teachers arrive before their students to make sure all the final preparations for the day are done. They duplicate tests, set up projects, and decorate bulletin boards. When the students arrive, teachers take attendance and collect lunch money. The rest of the day is spent instructing the children in different subjects, with the most time spent on reading and math. Teachers may also have to supervise lunchrooms, recesses, and bus loading.

The pleasures and pressures of the job

This is a great job if you love being around children all day. You will see how your lessons are motivating young children to learn. And there is so much delight in observing how students develop and learn during the year you spend with them.

Being an elementary school teacher isn't an easy job. You will be on your feet for many hours each day. You will not have too much contact with adults. On a bad day, teaching can drain your energy and challenge you to stay even-tempered.

The pay

How much money you make as an elementary school teacher depends largely on where you work. Do you think California, New York, Alaska, Pennsylvania, or Hawaii pays the highest salary for beginning teachers? If you picked Alaska, you are correct. In 1993 beginning teachers in Alaska were paid $40,905, which includes a cost-of-living adjustment. You can get local starting salary information from your State Department of Education or your school district. Teachers' salaries usually increase each year based on the number of years taught and educational degrees held.

Getting started

If you decide to become an elementary school teacher, you will have the opportunity to choose where you want to live and work. You can even teach in a foreign country. Although it is quite difficult to get a job in some areas at the present, the future appears brighter as many teachers are expected to retire or find other jobs.

To be an elementary school teacher you will need to have a college degree and meet the state license requirements. Part of your education will be as a student teacher in a classroom.

Climbing the career ladder

There are many other teachers besides classroom teachers in elementary schools. Today, most schools have reading teachers, speech teachers, music teachers, and physical education teachers. There are also teachers who work in gifted and talented programs and in special education. Some elementary school teachers become counselors, curriculum directors, and principals. There are also advisory positions within each State Department of Education.

Now decide if teaching elementary school is right for you

You probably have a good idea of what elementary school teachers do in the classroom. But do you know what you must do to prepare to teach just a single lesson and make it interesting?

Good preparation requires you to read textbooks, teacher's manuals, course-related materials, professional journals, and curriculum guides. Besides reading, you will have to get additional books, supplies, and materials for many lessons.

Things you can do to get a head start

Start now to prepare to get into a college that has a program for elementary school teachers. Check your schedule with your guidance counselor to make sure you are on the right track for the college of your choice. Besides taking the correct courses, you will need a certain grade point average for admission to college. You will also probably need to take a college admissions test in your senior year.

Let's Meet...

Karl Travis Knerr
Fifth Grade Teacher

Karl likes his job as fifth grade teacher because it has so much variety. He is a communicator, a planner, and a problem solver besides being a teacher.

What do you like most about your job?

There is no better feeling than achieving "small victories"—a child getting a perfect spelling paper for the first time or finally understanding how to figure the area of a rectangle.

Describe a typical day at work.

I begin my day be greeting each student. We prepare for the day and listen to the morning announcements. Students then move on to their special subjects. While the students are at specials, I prepare lessons and activities, grade papers, communicate with parents, and meet with other professionals and the principal. We work on math and language arts before lunch and science, health, and social studies in the afternoon. Sometime during the day, I always read aloud to my class. After saying good-bye to my class, I prepare the classroom for the next day and grade papers. Then I travel to the high school to coach track.

What do you like least about your job?

Many times teachers simply do not receive the appreciation they deserve. People do not seem to realize the sacrifice and effort teachers make to accomplish our vital job—education young people.

If you could start over, would you choose a different career?

No, I would choose teaching. When I wake up each morning, I know that I will be the rare person who goes to a job that truly makes me happy.

What is the most difficult part of your job?

The most difficult part of teaching for me is saying good-bye to my students at the end of the school year. After getting to know the children and helping them grow, I am both happy and sad to see them leave.

What first attracted you to teaching?

I have always enjoyed working with young people. During high school, I coached several elementary basketball and track teams. These experiences made me realize that teaching and working with young people is very rewarding.

Do you use what you learned in school on the job?

I am constantly using knowledge and skills from both my undergraduate and graduate classes as well as those gained during student teaching. Of course, nothing can take the place of on-the-job learning.

Karl's First Day on the Job

The first day of teaching my very own class was so exciting that I'll never forget it. I had spent long hours preparing my classroom. I had developed both long- and short-term goals for the coming school year. Everything that needed to be done had been done. Still, I had a difficult time sleeping the night before.

On the first day, I arrived at school long before the students. I greeted my new students with a smile and a friendly hello. I still remember their big eyes and unsure looks. Soon the children were smiling, and I felt wonderful. Many parents walked their sons and daughters to the classroom door. One mother informed me that her daughter was very shy and nervous about having her first man teacher. I assured her that we were going to have a wonderful year. I turned to the small second grader, smiled, and greeted her. She proceeded to throw up on my shoes. I cleaned my shoes and began my teaching career. I still stay in contact with many of the students from my first year of teaching. We exchange letters and cards, and I have attended their college and high school basketball games.

Let's Meet...

Rolando Quintana
First Grade Teacher

Rolando has taught young children in first, second, and third grades during his 14 years as a teacher. His strength lies in helping Mexican-American children succeed in school.

Describe a typical day at work.

I arrive when the children are getting off the bus around 7:45 because I have done all my preparation for the day the previous afternoon. I never leave school before 5, and I have been known to stay at school as late as 10:30. During the day, my lessons are flexible, but I make sure that I always cover the most important areas of reading and math.

Describe your work environment.

My classroom is designed to meet the needs of my children. I do have lots of manipulatives, which are objects the children can handle. My classroom is well decorated with things hanging from the ceiling and posters everywhere.

What advice would you give to young people starting out in teaching?

I would encourage minorities to go into education because it is a

rewarding career. It is also a good stepping
stone to other careers related to education.

What special aptitudes do you need to be a good first grade teacher?

A first grade teacher must be a bit of an actor.
You should also be a person who is spontaneous, patient, self-motivated, and a self-starter.
You need to be open-minded and willing to try
new things. And of course, you should be
excited about what you are doing.

Is there a lot of competition for jobs in elementary teaching?

Yes, competition in my area is keen so you
have to be exceptional to get a job. During
their school years, future teachers should
make sure they get experiences that others
don't have. For example, take more math
courses, become a computer expert, or get an
administration background.

What does the multi-cultural child need in school?

Today's society is mobile, and many children
are bilingual. Teachers have to help these
children so they can adapt and grow in the
classroom.

Do you recommend any early special train-ing for future teachers?

If you are thinking about being a teacher, you
should try to get as much experience as you
can inside the classroom. One way to pick up
teaching skills is to become a teacher's
assistant.

Favorite Things, Least Favorite Things

I like my job when:

- A light bulb goes on in my students' heads, and they really understand a concept that I have been teaching.

- Children say, "I like you as a teacher."

- I get a letter of appreciation from a parent at the end of the year (these letters are worth all my effort even if I only get one).

- I have time off as it allows me as a teacher to explore new areas and gives me time to go back to school.

I dislike my job when:

- Parents don't give teachers a chance and base their judgment about them on hearsay.

- I feel I am watched more than other teachers because I am different—I am Hispanic.

- I have to prove myself to be 10 times better than the other teachers in the building.

- There is no parent participation.

- Parents don't make sure that homework is done or spend any quality time with their children.

Success Stories

Elizabeth D. Koontz

Elizabeth Koontz started in the education field by creating special education programs for handicapped and retarded children in the North Carolina school system. She went on to receive her master's degree and also did additional graduate work at Columbia and Indiana universities. When the National Education Association changed its policies and accepted teachers of all races, she became active in the organization. In 1968, she became the first black educator ever to be elected NEA president and fought hard through the organization to improve education. In her inaugural address, she warned that teachers wanted a voice in decisions that affected education and also wanted to have job security and other benefits. In 1969, Elizabeth Koontz was appointed director of the Women's Bureau of the Department of Labor.

Armando M. Rodriguez

After being a teacher, administrator, and state consultant in California schools, Armando Rodriguez became the first chief of the Mexican Affairs Unit of the U.S. Office of Education in 1967. He was well suited for this job because of his own Mexican-American background and his experience as a public school teacher. He was well aware of the difficulties that Mexican-American children faced in getting a good education. Rodriguez felt that having more bilingual teachers would help Mexican-American children overcome the language barrier and that these children needed to be taught their own cultural background. In 1970 he became director of the Office for Spanish Speaking American Affairs for the U.S. Office of Education, where he continued to work to make school districts aware of the need for special programs for Mexican-American children.

Find Out More

You and elementary school teaching

As an elementary school teacher you will be required to be a . . .

disciplinarian, making sure the children follow the set rules.

team player, working with other teachers and staff members in your school building.

listener, hearing what the children in your class are saying about their problems.

referee, solving problems that occur between students.

motivator, encouraging students to acquire knowledge.

performer, grabbing and keeping the attention of your class as you teach each lesson throughout the day.

jack of all trades, having to teach music, art, physical education, and other subjects beyond the basics to your class.

lunchroom or playground monitor, making sure that everyone is orderly.

JUNIOR HIGH OR MIDDLE SCHOOL TEACHER

As a junior high or middle school teacher, you help children bridge the gap between childhood and adolescence. Because your students are changing so rapidly, you need to possess the skills of both elementary and high school teachers. At times your students will require the help and guidance of an elementary school teacher. At the same time, you must help your students become responsible independent learners. Your time with most students will probably be brief, as junior high and middle school teachers usually teach only one subject or related subjects like high school teachers do.

29

What it's like to be a junior high or middle school teacher

You will be able to teach a specialized subject area that truly interests you. Furthermore, you will have considerable knowledge of this area from your college courses. If you are a history buff, you can spend your entire day discussing the Revolutionary War or Napoleon with your students. Your class will be made up of students who are exuberant, full of energy, and high on life. One moment they will act mature, and the next they will be immature and unsettled. You will find it very satisfying to help them discover how to make the right choices—putting them on the road to success in school and their lives. You won't work with students just in class but also in school-sponsored activities.

Let's find out what happens on the job

You will do the same routine bookkeeping tasks that elementary teachers do. Now, however, you will find yourself doing tasks like taking attendance not just once a day but for every class. You will also write lesson plans for each class, make and correct tests, collect homework, and contact parents when it is necessary. You are more likely to give lectures on a topic then elementary school teachers, and you will expect your students to take notes. You will not be providing answers for every question; instead, you will be expecting your students to search out information for themselves. Your day will usually be divided into six to eight periods with a free period to prepare for your classes.

The pleasures and pressures of the job

It is a pleasure to be able to teach one subject that you truly enjoy all day long. And it is delightful to see how much your students change and grow up during the school year and to be part of helping them become more mature.

On the other hand, you will definitely not find it easy working with students who are trying to discover who they are and where they are going. At times these students can be difficult to control in the classroom. Furthermore, you don't get to know individual students as well as you would like because they spend such a brief time in your classroom each day.

Getting started

During your senior year in college you will spend much of your time looking for a job. The easiest way to find out which school districts are looking for teachers is to go to your college placement or career office. There you will find information about jobs as well as sign-up sheets for actual interviews. You can also contact school districts to find out if they are looking for teachers in your special area. Many teachers also find jobs by attending job fairs for teachers, through answering ads in newspapers and professional journals, by doing a superior job at a school as a student teacher, or from receiving job leads from college professors, teachers, and friends.

Climbing the career ladder

Teachers in junior high and middle schools can become department heads. As a department head, you would be responsible for all the teachers teaching the same general subject such as English, math, or science. You would work with the teachers to decide what is to be taught in each class and help them with any problems. And you also might be involved in rating the teacher's performance.

With further education, you can become a guidance counselor, school psychologist, remedial reading teacher, or administrator.

Now decide if teaching junior high or middle school is right for you

Think about the teachers that you have right now in junior high or middle school. Would you like to do their job? Do you feel that any of them are doing an outstanding teaching job? Is one teacher making his or her class so exciting and challenging that you can't wait to get to it each day? Are you really learning because of this teacher? If so, you should nominate that teacher to become your state's Teacher of the Year by getting an application from your State Department of Education. Then if you become a teacher like this exceptional teacher, one of your students may nominate you for this outstanding honor one day in the future.

Things you can do to get a head start

You should try to be around children who are 10 to 14 years old to make sure this is the age group you would really like to teach. Volunteer for scouting, sports, and club activities that will let you see if you can handle children this age. Tutor to gain experience in teaching and to get a better understanding of what it means to work with junior high and middle school students. Being a lifeguard can be a great job; it gives you the responsibility of handling this age group as well as teaching them swimming and water safety.

Let's Meet...

Kathy Lattimer
French and English Teacher

Kathy taught French and English in a middle school for nine years and is now chairman of the foreign language department for the middle school and high school.

Tell me how you got started in teaching?

Like many foreign language teachers, a trip to France excited me about my subject. My interest in teaching French came later. My desire to head the foreign language department followed years of heading projects and committees to develop new materials and ways of teaching foreign languages.

Did you need any special schooling or training?

I needed 4 years of college to earn my teaching license. To get good teaching jobs, I had to take additional courses over the years, attend professional conferences, and travel periodically to France and other French-speaking countries.

What special skills do you need to be a good teacher?

To be a good teacher you need to have a knowledge of your subject area, and understanding of how to teach it to others, and a great deal of patience.

What do you like most about your job?

Working with many different people, having the freedom to experiment with different ways of teaching, and spending my days in such a variety of activities.

What do you like least about your job?

What I like least about my job is the time I spend on schoolwork on evenings and weekends when I would like to be with my family. I often must grade papers, plan lessons, or call substitute teachers when I would rather be doing family activities.

Do you work alone or as part of a team?

Much of my job is done as part of a team. I work with parents and teachers to help students who are not doing well. I work with groups of teachers or other administrators to develop new ways of teaching and to handle matters such as discipline or attendance.

What is the most difficult part of your job?

The most difficult part of my job as department head is to work with one or two teachers who are not doing a very good job and do not see a need to change how they teach. This is especially difficult if their students are very unhappy and expect me to change things quickly.

Kathy Lattimer's Day

6:30   Arrive at school. Go through mail and use copy machine, if needed.

7:00   Chat with teachers in department as they arrive. Help or answer questions as needed.

7:30   Talk to technician in foreign language center. Discuss any special needs of the day.

8:00   Do final preparation for teaching my two classes. (Most people in my position teach four classes but do not have all my administrative duties.)

8:30-10:30   Teach two classes.

10:30   Check mailbox. Respond to phone messages, speak to counselor, order materials, et cetera.

11:30   Eat lunch.

12:00   Have a conference with a teacher whose class I am going to observe.

1:00   Observe the teacher teach a class.

2:00   Write a test; type the department newsletter; have a conference with a teacher, student or parent; or attend an administrative meeting.

3:00   Tutor a student or give a make-up test.

3:45   Leave school.

7:30-9:00   Plan classes for the next day.

Let's Meet...

Titus Exum
Eighth Grade American History Teacher

Titus is starting his 10th year as a teacher. He has taught both sixth and eighth grades.

How did you learn to value education?

While growing up during full segregation, we African-American students were taught that education was the key to success. Graduation from high school was an accomplishment, but a college degree would open doors with pay that high school graduates and dropouts could never experience. I believe that education is and will always be the key to success.

What is a successful teaching day?

A successful day for me is to have the students in my five classes actively participate in a class or group project, a class discussion, or a multilevel assignment. Then I can see the students actually learning in my classes. On a successful day, I am a monitor encouraging group work or listening.

Tell me about your first day of school each year.

The first day of school is just plain rough for all middle school students and their teachers. One must simply be a wave and go with the flow. Schedules are being changed, students go to the wrong teacher, new students are lost, old students want to relive the summer months in one visit, and two or three students have the same first and last names. And if this isn't difficult enough, you are also handling locker assignments, enrollment forms, school bus schedules, plus students who are asking to call home. Finally, the day ends, and a new school year has begun.

What are the most frustrating things about your job?

Too m any people outside the classroom are making decisions for teachers without consulting them. This includes political groups, boards of education, state departments of education, and civil rights groups, just to name a few. It is also very frustrating when administrators do not support teachers in disagreements between parents and teachers.

Do you work alone or as part of a team?

I work on a five-person team. Each teacher teaches only one subject; however, we work together to plan assemblies, arrange field trips, discuss student behavior problems, select guest speakers, organize field days, and handle other situations involving all of the eighth grade teachers.

Titus' Resume

When teachers like Titus Exum apply for a job, they often submit resumes, which describe their qualifications. This resume gives Titus' background before he took his present job.

Titus Exum

Education:

Lincoln University, Jefferson City, Missouri
M.S., School Administration and Supervision, 1973
B.S., Elementary Education, 1968

Experience:

1976–1987   U.S. Army Transportation Corps
Entered service as a second lieutenant, retired as a captain.

1973–1975   Weeks Elementary School, Kansas City, Missouri
Sixth grade teacher

Certification:

Elementary teaching credentials
Missouri and Alaska

Success Stories

Mary McLeod Bethune may have spent her early years as a field hand picking cotton, but she grew up to become a forceful spokeswoman for black education and integration. When she was 29, she opened a school for black girls in Daytona Beach, Florida. Later, this school joined with a boys school to become a college with Bethune as its president.

During her lifetime, Bethune was appointed by five presidents to important government posts. As the director of the Division of Negro Affairs of the National Youth Administration, she became the first black woman to head a federal agency. In 1935, she received the Spingarn medal from the National Association for the Advancement of Colored People for her contributions to black education.

John Dewey

What you do in school today has been greatly influenced by John Dewey. Before Dewey, educators believed that students should learn by memorizing what their teachers told them to learn. Dewey opposed this idea and said that learning should be related to the interests of students and what was happening in the world. He also thought that learning should not just be connected with the mind but should include a student's physical and moral well-being.

Dewey was born in 1859 and lived to be almost 100. He taught at several universities and saw his new educational philosophy widely accepted.

Find Out More

You and junior high or middle school teaching

Note all the tasks involved in getting a job as a junior high or middle school teacher.

1. *Completing an application for state certification.*
   You will need to supply information about citizenship, health, age, and moral character. You will also need to have a bachelor's degree. And you may need to have taken special courses in state history.

2. *Taking the National Teacher Examination.*

   Many states require you to pass the NTE to get a teaching certificate. School districts may also require you to pass this test in order to get a job.

3. *Taking a competency teat in basic skills or a subject area.*

   In certain states, you may be required to pass a competency test to get a teaching position.

4. *Completing an application for employment.*

   You will need to complete a separate application for every school district to which you apply.

5. *Creating a resume.*

   Besides completing an application, almost everyone applying for a teaching job creates a personal resume, which tells about her or his education, job experiences, and special skills.

6. *Putting together a credentials file for the college placement file.*

   Your credentials file will include a personal data sheet and letters of reference. It may also include a record of your grades in college.

Find out more about junior high or middle school teaching

By now you have probably discovered that teaching is a career that requires a lot of reading. The following books will help you learn more about what the teaching profession is really like.

Milgram, Gail Cleason. *Your Future in Education.* New York: Richards Rosen Press Inc., 1979.

Ramsey, Patricia. *Teaching Multi-Cultural Education.* New York: Teachers College Press, 1987.

Teaching in America: The Common Ground. New York: Yale University Press, 1985.

HIGH SCHOOL TEACHER

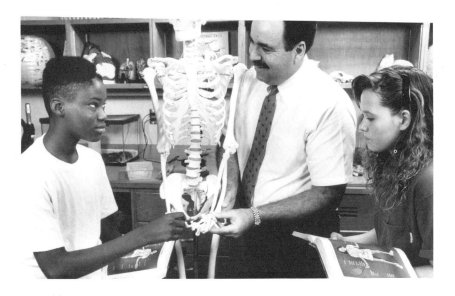

High school teachers share their knowledge of a favorite subject such as math, history, astronomy, Spanish, or music with their students. They also work closely with their students in extracurricular activities. For example, you could teach English all day, and then work for weeks after school helping the drama club produce a play. Or you might find yourself teaching five classes of biology and then coaching the girls' volleyball team. No matter what you like to do, a high school teaching job will let you share your personal interests with your students.

What it's like to be a high school teacher

You will probably be teaching all your classes in the same subject area; however, few high school teachers teach the same class all day long. A science teacher may teach both chemistry and physics, and an art teacher may have both drawing and craft classes. You will usually stay in the same classroom all day and have five classes lasting from 40 to 55 minutes. Most high school teachers have a free period that can be used to prepare for their classes. Besides duties directly related to teaching, you may find yourself supervising a homeroom, a study hall, or a lunchroom. And considerable time will be spent conferring with students and parents, participating on various committees, chaperoning and supervising school functions, and directing extracurricular activities.

Let's find out what happens on the job

You will need to make sure that the students in your classes learn the material. To do that you will have to create lessons that meet the varied learning styles of everyone in a class. Teachers check their students' progress through analyzing written and oral work, asking questions, and grading quizzes and tests. Records must be kept of each student's progress. Teachers use this information in making out report cards and discussing how students are doing with their parents, counselors, and the students themselves.

The pleasures and pressures of the job

One of the pleasures of being a high school teacher is working with students who are generally more independent, sophisticated, and self-reliant than younger students. Furthermore, most high school students understand the importance of doing well in school.

Don't consider being a high school teacher if you expect to be home right after school each day. Teachers have other obligations besides teaching. They are also expected to do their share of supervising the lunchroom, bus loading, and the halls, and chaperoning after-school events. They also must attend department and faculty meetings regularly.

The pay

According to the National Education Association, public high school teachers averaged more than $30,000 a year in the early 1990s. Pay will usually increase each year according to a district's salary schedule. Salaries in private schools are usually lower.

In many high schools, teachers get extra pay for working with students in extracurricular activities such as sports, publications, and clubs. Some teachers earn additional income by teaching summer school.

Getting started

You can gain valuable teaching experience from these activities:

Become a tutor. Talk to your guidance counselor or a teacher in a subject in which you excel to find out how you can get on the school's list of tutors. You might also want to gain experience tutoring junior high or middle school students.

Become a teacher's assistant. Many high schools have programs in which students have the opportunity to work for a teacher helping to set up equipment, grading papers, and doing other clerical jobs. Some schools even give credits for participating in this program.

Now decide if high school teaching is right for you

High school teachers have a wide variety of duties. Are you willing to . . .

work more than 40 hours each week?

take papers home to grade?

help students both before and after school almost every day?

present material in different ways to meet the needs of individual students?

take college classes to keep up-to-date in your field?

attend conferences to bring back more information to your students?

spend considerable time preparing for each class?

prepare in the summer to make each year a better one?

get a bachelor's degree and a master's degree?

answer parents' questions when you meet them in a shopping center?

receive phone calls from parents in the evening at your home?

get involved in helping students with nonacademic problems?

Let's Meet...

Thomas Dick
Orchestra Teacher

Thomas' goal is to give his students a good experience in his orchestra classes, which he hopes will lead to a lifetime of enjoying good music and playing a musical instrument.

Tell me how you got started in teaching.

I really remember a startled awareness during my senior year of college that I wanted to help young people prepare themselves for life. It was like a calling. From that time on, everything seemed to fall in place.

Describe a typical day at work.

There is no typical day when you work with today's youth. We do spend a lot of time in rehearsals preparing for concerts. My day is long. Four days a week, I supervise rehearsals of different sections of the orchestra after school. Then every Tuesday evening, I hold a 3-hour rehearsal of performance and possible contest pieces to discover problems that the students can work on at home and in their sections.

How did you feel when you got your first job?

Elated, relieved. I must say, at this point, that I have never sought a teaching position. I have had the good fortune to be recruited for each job.

What is the most difficult part of your job?

It is difficult to say goodbye to seniors who have been a part of the high school orchestra program for 3 years.

What special skills do you need to be a good teacher?

- Knowledge of the subject matter
- An ability to relate to the students
- Patience
- Love for your students

What is a typical class?

During a typical strings class, I will begin by having the students play scales for intonation, quality of sound, and technique. Most of the period will be devoted to working on problems with current pieces with some time devoted to sight reading and the teaching of musical terms, abbreviations, and signs.

Tell me about your first day at work.

I was a very confident person until I stepped into the classroom for the first time. Then I was in awe of the responsibility.

A Tribute to Thomas

When Thomas left his last job for his present position, his orchestra students wrote this tribute to him.

A Tribute to the Conductor

As our teacher, we have both loved and admired him, for he has been much more than a simple instructor. Not only has he been the key to our musical growth, but he has been our friend and our inspiration as well. Through him we have been encouraged to better ourselves both with music and in our daily lives.

As our conductor, he has shared with us his wonderful gift of music. Through his help and guidance we have each been allowed to develop our inner talents into a product that we can use to bring joy to others.

As our friend, he has gone beyond what is expected of him as a teacher. He has been our smile on a cloudy day and our encouragement to carry on. His pride in both our triumphs and our failures has been heartfelt, for he showed us that there is more to life than merely winning, just as there is more to music than simple notes.

With all that he means to us, his departure brings us great sadness. However, as we realize that his purpose is to continue to touch the lives of others, we can only hope that he leaves here knowing how much he has enriched our lives through the benefits of his teachings.

Let's Meet...

William Duke
High School Principal

William started his career in education 26 years ago as a teacher. Now he is principal of a large suburban high school.

What jobs did you have before becoming a principal?

I climbed up every step on the administrative career ladder to become a principal when I was 40. I began by teaching mathematics for 9 years at a middle school. I was happy teaching. However, because of my organizational skills, I was offered the position of athletic director, which launched my career in the field of administration. I went on to working in the attendance office. For 10 years, I was an assistant principal before becoming a principal.

Is being an administrator a full-time job?

Being an administrator is a 12-month-a-year job. Of course, you do get vacation days. But because the volume of work is so great, if you take off too much time you will find it difficult to catch up, especially on all the paperwork.

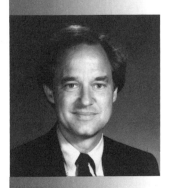

What is the most difficult part of your job?

Dealing with unnecessary conflicts, dealing with a misinformed public, and changing the public perception of education.

Describe one of your happiest moments on the job.

I am a people person, and I want all the students at my school to feel special about their high school experience. I am truly happy when I am able to get the students and the staff charged up about learning. I find it exciting to watch them grow.

Describe your work environment.

Busy, rather exciting, fun, energetic, and positive.

What special skills do you need to be a good principal?

Communication, being accessible, decisiveness, being visible, and predictability.

Did you need any special schooling or training?

Yes, I have a bachelor's degree in math. Then to go into administration, I obtained a master's degree in education and my administrative license. I also went back to the university and got my educational specialist degree and doctorate in school administration so that I would know more about how children learn. It is absolutely essential today for teachers to keep current so extra schooling is always going to be required.

A Typical Day at Work as a Principal

In my job I never have a typical day. Every day is different, and that is why I like my job. I find myself doing things that I had not even planned on doing. Nevertheless. I keep a "do list" and chip away at it each day.

I arrive in the building around 7 A.M. and spend the time before school starts walking around talking to the teachers and students. I like to be visible to everyone. Then I usually have administrative meetings with the different directors and deans. I spend lunch hour in the cafeteria again being visible to everybody in the building. From 3:30 to 5:30 is the most productive time of day for me as I am able to work without interruption on things that need to get done. Three or four nights a week, I return to school to attend games, performing arts events, awards banquets, school board meetings, and committee meetings.

I took this job as principal because I am a people person. Administration is a service occupation. I really do enjoy watching the students in my school at all the different events. I find it very relaxing because I am not required to do anything but be supportive at functions that I truly enjoy.

Success Stories

Christa McAuliffe

The first "ordinary person" selected by NASA to participate in a space shuttle mission was teacher Christa McAuliffe. She was selected from more than 11,000 other teachers not because of her scientific knowledge, but because she was an exceptional high school teacher. Christa's mission was to conduct two 15-minute classes on closed-circuit television from space for millions of students back on earth. However, Christa McAuliffe was not able to conduct her lessons from outer space. Just 73 seconds after lift-off, the shuttle exploded, killing everyone on board.

Lyndon Baines Johnson

Lyndon Baines Johnson taught public speaking and debate at a high school in Houston, Texas, after he graduated from college. Lyndon loved teaching but felt that he would be able to help more people if he went into politics. He became a member of the House of Representatives and then a senator, vice president, and president. As president, Lyndon improved the nation's educational system, and Congress passed his proposals for more federal aid to education.

Find Out More

You and high school teaching

See if you can answer the following questions about being a high school teacher. If you can, then you probably know enough about teaching at this level to make a decision on the suitability of a high school teaching career for yourself.

1. What are the main duties of a high school teacher?

2. Why do high school teachers have to spend so much time after school and on weekends working at school?

3. What degrees and licenses do high school teachers need?

4. What are you doing right now to see if high school teaching is a good career choice for you?

5. Describe a typical work day for a high school teacher.

6. Is there a subject or subjects that are so absorbing that you would like to teach them? If so, what are they?

**Find out
more about
high school
teaching**

You can find out more about teaching at all levels, including high
school, by contacting the following
organizations.

National Education Association of
   the United States
1202 16th St. N.W.
Washington, DC 20036

Department of Public Relations
American Federation of Teachers
11 Dupont Circle N.W.
Washington, DC 20036

COLLEGE

TEACHER

As a teacher at a college or university, you will be teaching and advising some of the more than 13 million full-time and part-time students at schools of higher education. You may be teaching students how to become doctors, lawyers, teachers, or engineers, or you could be teaching them about Shakespeare, the Roman Empire, or the geography of South America. No matter what you teach, you will truly be an expert in that subject. And your days will be devoted to learning more about the subject you teach.

What it's like to be a college teacher

You will be teaching bright, eager students who want to learn. Most will be recent high school graduates. They will ask challenging questions and expect you to have the answers. To keep up with what is happening in your subject, you are going to spend much of your time doing research. This means a lot of time devoted to reading books and papers and studying reports. You will also have the opportunity to travel to conferences and meetings to find out what others in your field are doing and to share your work with them. You will probably be the author of several books and numerous papers during your career. You may even write the textbook for one of your classes.

Let's find out what happens on the job

The size of the college or university makes a great difference in how a teacher handles a class. At a large university, you might not even be standing in front of your class but instead be lecturing to them via closed-circuit television. Most universities are on the semester schedule, so you will teach two semesters and usually have the summers free to pursue other interests or teach summer school. You will be teaching two to four classes each semester, and the classes will meet one to five times a week. You will teach mostly by lecturing, but you will also have small discussion groups. Besides teaching, you will spend much of your time advising students, researching, writing papers and books, and being a consultant for businesses and the government.

The pleasures and pressures of the job

One of the great pleasures for college teachers is being able to take a sabbatical, a year or a shorter period when teachers are free of teaching responsibilities to pursue their interests. Some spend this time doing research or writing a book. Others like to travel and study. Teachers will usually receive a full or partial salary from their schools while they are on sabbatical.

The greatest pressure on college teachers is having to publish papers, reports, and books on their research. If they fail to publish, they may not be able to advance in their profession.

Getting started

To become a college teacher, you really need to love learning and going to school. You will not find many college teachers who have not graduated from college and spent several years in graduate school. To become an assistant professor at a 4-year college, you will almost always need to have both master's and doctoral degrees. It usually takes from 1 to 2 years to get a master's.

Then you will need to study from 3 to 7 or more years to get a doctorate.

Climbing the career ladder

The usual entry teaching position at college is as an assistant professor. Then the effort begins to get tenure, which is permanent status as a faculty member. During the trial years before tenure is granted, a period of 7 to 10 years, assistant professors struggle to make names for themselves. The usual way to do this is by publishing papers. This is the reason for the expression "publish or perish."

During this trial period, you will spend every spare minute reading as you research to write your papers. You will become an associate professor when you get tenure. Then after many years, you may become a full professor. Perhaps you will go on to become a department chairperson or college administrator.

Now decide if college teaching is right for you

If you have the following skills, you'd probably make a good teacher.

First, if you like working with people and helping them learn, you'd probably make a good teacher. Become a college teacher if you want to work with young adults.

Second, if you like being an expert on a subject, you'd probably make a good teacher. Become a college teacher if you want to become an expert in a narrow field.

Third, if you like to plan learning experience so others understand a subject, you'd probably make a good teacher. Become a college teacher if you would like to teach through lecturing.

Fourth, if you like to communicate with others, you'd probably make a good teacher. Become a college teacher if you like talking to young adults.

Things you can do to get a head start

If you are going to be a college teacher, you are going to need to know how to study. After 4 years of college, you will have to get both a master's and a doctorate degree. This will mean at least 8 years of schooling after high school. Check to see if you have learned how to study effectively.

____ I always meet deadlines.

____ I budget my time.

____ I set up a study schedule and follow it.

____ I know how to use research tools.

____ I know how to take good notes.

____ I know how to study for tests.

Let's Meet...

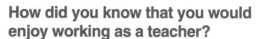

James Riley
Mathematics Teacher

James has taught 9,876 students in 323 classes during his 34 years of teaching mathematics. He taught one year in high school and the past 33 years at a university.

How did you know that you would enjoy working as a teacher?

I always enjoyed learning. It does not make any difference whether the topic happens to be music, art, science, government, economics, business, or sports. I always found joy in working with children, and I got satisfaction in helping others learn.

Is there a lot of competition for jobs teaching in college?

There is a great deal of competition for jobs. It is no longer as easy to get into the profession as it was when I started. This year we had a job opening in our department. We had more than 100 applications.

Describe your work environment.

In a word, freedom. Other than the requirement of meeting my classes and submitting some paperwork (like grades), I am left completely alone. I am free to pursue whatever interests me.

Describe one of your happiest moments on the job.

The happiest moments for me come at unexpected times and places. It happens when I am stopped in a restaurant or in a mall by a middle-age person who says something like "You're Dr. Riley, aren't you? I had you for a math class 20 years ago, and it was the best class I ever had. I am still teaching and I make the kids work as hard as you made us work."

How many classes do you teach?
How much preparation is required?

I always teach three classes a term. Most professors only teach two classes. I teach three because I enjoy the teaching and would feel cheated with anything less. The three classes put me in the classroom 10 to 12 hours a week. I spend about 1 hour outside of class in preparation for each hour in class. In addition, I spend about half an hour for each hour in class correcting papers.

Trace your career path.

I graduated from college and was called to active duty in the U.S. Army for 4 years. When I left the Army, I enrolled in a master's program and taught mathematics at a local high school.

One year later, I was offered a temporary position as a mathematics instructor at the university while I completed my master's degree. Since I received my doctorate, I have been at the university rising through the ranks. I will stay here until I retire. It is a good life.

James Visits Holland

After I completed my doctorate degree, I was granted a year's leave to travel to the Netherlands to investigate its mathematics education system. This activity was centered at the University of Utrecht's Institute of Mathematics Education. The director of the Institute was the world-renowned mathematician Hans Fruedenthal. I spent the year visiting teacher training institutions, schools, and professional meetings.

One day, I was invited to attend a conference on mathematics education sponsored by the Institute. During the day, our time was taken up by meetings, presentations, and discussions. At dinner I was fortunate to have been assigned to sit at Professor Fruedenthal's table. However, Professor Fruedenthal would not let us eat until we had solved a problem. Can you solve it?

Karl and Jan met after many years. After an exchange of greetings, Jan asked, "Karl, are you married?"

"Oh, yes, " replied Karl, "and I have three sons."

"Wonderful!" exclaimed Jan. "And what are their ages?"

"The product of their ages is 72," answered Karl.

"But that doesn't answer my question," Jan protested.

"Well, the sum of their ages is the same as your house number," Karl added.

"I still don't know their ages," Jan complained.

"The oldest boy plays chess," Karl offered.

"Now I know their ages," Jan responded.

What are the sons' ages?

* For the answer, look on page 70.

Let's Meet...

Maxine J. Pijiaux
Director of Program for Preparing School Principals

Maxine has worked in a variety of educational positions. She has been a teacher, a principal, an assistant and associate superintendent, and a superintendent.

What first attracted you to a career in education?

It was my interest in children that attracted me to education plus my desire to increase their skills, knowledge, and understanding of themselves and others. And I wanted to help them learn more about their political, social, and economic environment.

Is a career in education something you always dreamed of?

Yes, as a child I always played school. And when I did, I always had to be the teacher. Many of my elementary and high school teachers, served as role models for me. I wanted to emulate them in a teaching career.

How did you know you would enjoy working as an educator?

I genuinely enjoy people and have always helped others. Therefore, I saw teaching as a career that would permit me to assist others and bring out the best in people.

How did you get started in education?

I began my career as a fifth grade classroom teacher before I became an administrator and then a college teacher.

Did you need any special schooling or training for your different jobs?

I have been required to get several degrees. First of all, to be an elementary school teacher, I had to have a bachelor's degree in education. To serve as a administrator, I needed to get a master's in educational administration and supervision. To become a college teacher, I needed a doctorate in educational administration and supervision. I also have a master's in business administration. This degree was not required for any of my jobs, but it is very helpful when I am involved in management and finance.

Describe a typical day at work.

There is never a typical day. Each day brings new and different events—some planned and some unexpected.

What special skills do you need to be a good college teacher in your area?

Extensive knowledge of educational administration, practical, firsthand experience, excellent listening skills, and excellent oral and written communication skills.

How Maxine Got Her Job

This is the process that Dr. Pijiaux followed in finding out about, applying for, and interviewing for her current job.

Finding out about jobs

1. Reviewed job listings in local, state, and national publications.

Applying for jobs

1. Selected jobs I wanted to apply for.
2. Sent a letter of interest and a resume to prospective employers and asked for a job application.
3. Completed and returned the job applications with my list of references.

Handling the job interview

1. Made certain that my appearance was good.
2. Had knowledge of the job.
3. Listened attentively.
4. Answered questions clearly.
5. Stayed focused.

Success Stories

Barbara Jordan

Barbara Jordan has come a long way from her humble beginning in a poor neighborhood to become a state legislator and the South's first black U.S. congresswoman. Barbara spent 6 highly visible years in the House of Representatives from 1973 to 1978. After she left public office, she became a professor at the University of Texas in Austin.

As a professor, Jordan does a great amount of preparation. Her classes are always crowded and admission to her lectures is done by a lottery system. She loves her teaching job and wants all of her students to be premier public servants who have a core of principles to guide them. "They are my future and the future of this country," she explains.

Theodore Hesburgh

Under his leadership as president of Notre Dame University, Father Hesburgh made Notre Dame a model for other universities. As president, he reduced his own power and gave more power to the college teachers. Father Hesburgh has been the director of many different educational societies and a member of the U.S. Commission on Civil Rights.

Find Out More

Reasons for choosing a career as a college teacher

Study the following reasons individuals have chosen college teaching as their careers. If you agree with more statements than you disagree, you should investigate further a career as a college teacher.

I would like to study throughout my life.

I want to be challenged intellectually every day.

I am very attracted to a particular subject.

I enjoy doing research.

I want to associate with young adults.

I want to contribute to the development of the next generation.

I am intrigued with the learning process.

I value the intellectual freedom a college teacher has.

I like doing my preparation, research, and reading whenever I wish.

I want to spend time with others who are experts in my subject area.

I want to counsel young people.

Find out more about college teaching

By writing to the following organizations, you can learn more about a career as a college teacher.

American Association of University
    Professors
1 Dupont Circle, Suite 500
Washington, DC 20036

American Association of State
    Colleges and Universities
1 Dupont Circle, Suite 700
Washington, DC 20036

National Education Association
1201 16th St. N.W.
Washington, DC 20036

Solution to riddle on page 64:

List all the factors of 72, in sets of 3 (one for each son).

Since the result does not answer Jan's question, even though at least one sum does equal his house number, there must be more than one sum that could be right. Only two sets of factors sum to the same number (14), so it must be one of those two.

Of the two similar sums, only one has a single largest number (oldest son).

The answer is 3, 3, and 8.

SPECIAL

EDUCATION

TEACHER

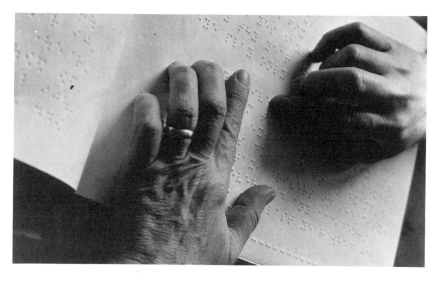

I magine being able to teach a deaf child to sign, an emotionally disturbed child to control anger, or a very gifted child to explore new ideas. As a special education teacher, you could be helping any of these students or those who are learning disabled, mentally retarded, visually impaired, or handicapped in some other way. This is a particularly rewarding career as you are providing valuable help to children that regular classroom teachers are not able to give them. As a special education teacher, you could give some student the boost that Annie Sullivan gave to Helen Keller.

What it's like to be a special education teacher

The children you teach will learn differently from most children in a typical classroom so you must discover how each child learns best and create individualized programs. You will have to be especially creative and resourceful to meet this challenge. Other specialists will help you figure out what to expect from each child. But you will have to gather the materials needed and provide the instruction your students need, whether they are handicapped in some way or gifted.

Let's find out what happens on the job

You will not be working alone; you may have an aide. You will also be working closely with regular classroom teachers, doctors, social workers, psychologists, speech pathologists, and parents to make sure that you have created the best individual learning plan for each child. Students may spend all or just part of a day with you. Your teaching will be as individualized as possible. You may have your own classroom or go to other teachers' classrooms to help one or more students. You can be teaching at the elementary, middle, junior or senior high school level, or even a combination of levels. Furthermore, special education teachers don't just work at schools; you could have a job at an institution or a residential center.

The pleasures and pressures of the job

Special education teachers get a lot of pleasure from their jobs because they are helping students with very special and real needs. There is immense satisfaction in helping a dyslexic child learn to read, a mentally retarded individual learn to dial a phone number, or a gifted child learn to use a special talent. There is stress from all the paperwork that special education teachers have to do to meet school and government requirements. And there is also pressure to keep up with all the laws that these teachers must follow and the latest educational ideas for helping their students. It is also stressful to deal all day with students who have such enormous needs.

Climbing the career ladder

You will need to meet your state's licensing requirements to become a special education teacher. Many states will require you to have certification in either elementary or secondary education as well as your special area. And there are even some states that require you to have graduate courses in your specialty.

Special education teachers can climb the career ladder to become supervisors and administrators. Approximately 50 percent of all the people working in special education are teachers. However, 14 percent are supervisors or directors and 4 percent are school administrators. There is also an opportunity to become a consultant or a researcher in special education, although there are not too many jobs in these areas.

Now decide if teaching special education is right for you

Find out in your school right now how many special education teachers there are. Remember that there are special education teachers for gifted and talented students as well as students who have physical or learning disabilities. Do you have the same traits as these teachers do?

Are you compassionate?

Are you hooked on helping those with special needs?

Are you patient?

Are you satisfied with making progress very slowly?

Do you enjoy spending time with children who are handicapped?

Do you prefer working with individuals and small groups?

Do you enjoy making detailed plans?

Can you handle paperwork smoothly?

Can you work effectively with other people?

Things you can do to get a head start

If you really feel that you would like to work in special education, you should volunteer to help with community projects involving people with special needs. Get experience working at Special Olympics or with organizations like Muscular Dystrophy Foundation. Tutor children at the public library who are having problems learning to read. Get associated with a camp for handicapped children.

Let's Meet...

Lysandra Walker
Teacher of the Deaf

Lysandra teaches communication skills to deaf students in elementary, middle, and high school. She also educates the teachers and administrators about the needs of her special students.

Is a career in deaf education something you always dreamed of?

No, I have always liked to help people, but I did not want to teach. I did not decide until I was in college that I wanted to teach children with a handicapping condition. The school I attended had a deaf education program, and one day I just skipped class and changed my major from special education to deaf education.

What do you like most about your job?

I have found that I can really make a difference in deaf education. I am able to see a child who had no way of communicating be able to really tell you something. I can see the benefits of my teaching efforts each day.

What do you like least about your job?

Students who really need to work with me can't because my caseload is so heavy that I don't have any free time to work with them.

Is there a lot of competition for jobs in deaf education?

No, there is actually a shortage of teachers of the deaf. Unfortunately, there is no medical cure for deafness at the present so there is a great need for teachers in this area. In addition, many deaf children are now in regular classrooms and need the special help of teachers of the deaf to do their work.

What special skills do you need to be a good teacher of the deaf?

You need to be patient because progress is very slow. And optimism also helps because the gains a deaf child make one day may not be there the next day. You will have to learn how to deal with children with varying degrees of deafness, which is quite difficult to do. Of course, the one skill most teachers of the deaf need is the ability to sign.

What advice would you give to young people starting out in deaf education?

Learn as much as you can about deafness and how to teach the deaf in your college courses. Don't expect your job to be easy. Deafness is the hardest sensory loss to overcome. You will be teaching children who can't communicate the way most people do. We learn so much through hearing what family, friends, and people on radio and television say. Deaf people can't learn in this way.

Daily Schedule

My schedule is quite confusing because I work with students in three separate schools: elementary, middle, and high school. Every day I am at two of these schools while I go to the middle school only twice a week. Some days it seems like I spend more time in the car dashing between schools than I do teaching.

7:30	Arrive at the elementary school and work the breakfast line.
8:15	Open classroom at school so children in my deaf classes can get the equipment they use in regular classes.
8:30 - 9:30	Teach a daily class of two students at the high school, and talk to their teachers about the extra help these students need.
10:20 - 11:20	Return to the elementary school, except on Tuesdays and Thursdays when I go to the middle school, and work with children on answering simple questions aloud.
11:30 - 1:00	Work on lesson plans in my classroom and break for lunch.
1:15	Work with my students at the elementary school in their regular classrooms.
2:15	Handle routine day-end duties such as putting kids on the bus.
2:35	End of school day.
3:00	Depart for home.

Let's Meet...

Judy Whiteman
Teacher of the Visually Impaired

Judy currently teaches Braille at the Indiana School for the Blind. She has also taught visually impaired children in grades four, five, and six.

What first attracted you to a career in teaching?

I was lucky enough to have a first grade teacher that I loved. She was very patient and kind. Ever since I started here at the Indiana School for the Blind at seven, I said, "I am going to be a teacher."

Do you think you are suited to the job?

Yes. This is a school where I truly have something to offer. When I teach, I am able to share insights with the children that sighted teachers are not able to because they have not lived in a blind world. A bond exists between me and the children. I help them when they are frustrated, especially teen-agers who feel that they do not get enough freedom from their families.

Describe your happiest moments on the job.

To me the happiest moments come when a child who has struggled

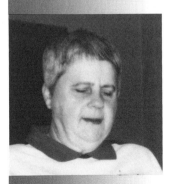

finally succeeds. Fortunately, for me, these happy moments occur frequently.

What difficulties did you face when you selected teaching as a career?

Several universities and colleges said they would not guarantee my receiving a recommendation for a teaching license even if I successfully completed the requirements. You need to remember that this happened back in the 1950s. The dean of the school of education tried to talk my father into getting me to change careers, but my father told him that if I believed that I could become a teacher, it was good enough for him.

Did you need any special help in college?

I had already learned typing skills so I could hand in my assignments. However, the books that I needed to read were not in Braille or on tape so I required readers. Readers are people who read textbook material to blind students.

What degrees and licenses do you have?

I have a bachelor's degree in elementary education and a master's degree in education. I have also taken additional classes in the special field of study for the blind to add an additional certification to my permanent general elementary teaching certificate.

How do you read?

I am an avid reader. I like to read the bestsellers, but they are not translated into Braille as quickly as I would like so I have been trained on an Optacon. This machine has changed my whole life.

A Sample Schedule—in Braille

What you see in the background is what this schedule would look like if it were typed in braille.

6:45   I arrive at school so that I can make final preparations for the day and review my lesson plans.

7:15 -   All the teachers have time for meetings,
7:45   grading papers, talking to other teachers, preparing materials.

The day at the Indiana School for the Blind is divided up into eight periods. The first one is a 28-minute advisory period. During this time each teacher works with three to five junior high and high school students assigned to them. The teachers will work with these same students until they graduate. The remaining seven periods are 50 minutes in length.

12:00   Teachers eat lunch.

12:30   Classes resume.

3:15   The teaching day is over, however, sometimes there are meetings after school for the teachers.

Success Stories

Annie Sullivan began her teaching career in Boston at the Perkins School for the Blind. However, she left the school and took on the challenging task of becoming the tutor to a 7-year-old girl named Helen Keller who was blind, deaf, and mute. Annie knew that she had to help Helen make a connection between letters traced on her hand and the object. The whole key to opening the world to Helen was in acquainting her with language. After only a month, Annie accomplished this task. Once Helen knew that everything had a name she kept her teacher busy teaching her hundreds of new words. Annie received praise from Alexander Graham Bell and even President Grover Cleveland for her fantastic work.

Alexander Melville Bell

Alexander Melville Bell taught deaf-mutes to speak and wrote textbooks on correct speech. In the mid-1880s, he created the pictorial alphabet to help deaf people learn to speak and read. The pictorial alphabet showed deaf people the proper mouth position for forming each letter sound. This alphabet revolutionized the way teachers of the deaf taught their students. Bell's work is explained in his book *Visible Speech: The Science of Universal Alphabetics,* which he wrote in 1867. Alexander was the father of Alexander Graham Bell, who invented the telephone. The younger Bell assisted his father in public demonstrations of visible speech and also became his father's partner in teaching the deaf.

Find Out More

You and teaching special education

Part of the task of getting a teaching job in any area is to be able to explain why you want it and why you are specially qualified for it. It is not too early for you to start creating a folder of information to use as background material for resumes, cover letters, and personal interviews. Then you can use this information when you are trying to get a job or work as a volunteer. Organizations will want the following information.

What experience have you had in working with or knowing children who have handicaps?

What jobs have you held?

Have you done volunteer work?

What are your special skills (typing, computer, language)?

What is your interest in helping the handicapped?

What is your grade point average? What courses are you studying?

Who would recommend you for a job? Include their addresses and phone numbers.

What do you see yourself doing in the future?

**Find out
more about
being a
special
education
teacher**

Use these three resources to begin
to find out more about special
education and the handicapped.

Association for Children and Adults
    with Learning Disabilities
4156 Library Road
Pittsburgh, PA 15234

The Council for Exceptional
    Children
1920 Association Drive
Reston, VA 22091–1589

Gallaudet University
Pre-College Programs
800 Florida Ave. N.W.
Washington, DC 20002

INDEX